Praise for *Integration Marketing*

"The most important book of the year."

—Codrut Turcanu
Founder of Remarkable Blogging
www.remarkableblogging.com

"Mark Joyner's new book *Rocks*!

After reading it yesterday evening, I put all other work on hold to create two Integration Marketing processes—and have been spreading the word about them.

Already, within 24 hours, I've started seeing Results.

And the way I've implemented [it] is rudimentary and basic. There are so many nuances to make it more powerful and effective.

To think so much wisdom and insight can be packed into such a short volume. . . . Wow!

I'm urging everyone I care about in a business sense to stop everything else and read *Integration Marketing* right now."

—Dr. Mani Sivasubramanian
www.DrMani.name

"I've read the book four times in one day. I gave my first lecture on *Integration Marketing* to my staff today—it generated incredible excitement."

—Alan Walter
CEO of Knowledgism
www.knowledgism.com

integration marketing

How Small Businesses Become Big Businesses—and Big Businesses Become Empires

MARK JOYNER

WILEY

JOHN WILEY & SONS, INC.

Published by John Wiley & Sons, Inc., Hoboken, New Jersey.
Published simultaneously in Canada.

For general information on our other products and services or for technical support, please contact our Customer Care Department within the United States at (800) 762-2974, outside the United States at (317) 572-3993 or fax (317) 572-4002.

Wiley also publishes its books in a variety of electronic formats. Some content that appears in print may not be available in electronic books. For more information about Wiley products, visit our web site at www.wiley.com.

Library of Congress Cataloging-in-Publication Data:

Joyner, Mark.
   Integration marketing : how small businesses become big businesses–
and big businesses become empires / Mark Joyner.
      p. cm.
   Include index.
   ISBN 978-0-470-45459-6 (cloth)
   1. Strategic planning.   2. Marketing.   3. Small business.   4. Big business.
I. Title.
   HD30.28.J694 2009
   658.8'01 — dc22

                                                              2008052031

Printed in the United States of America.

10   9   8   7   6   5   4   3   2   1

Hey, Where's the Fire?

(Please read this before proceeding. It's important. Really.)

This book is a short, easy read, with a very large payoff. By the time you've finished, you'll:

- Be equipped to find marketing opportunities that will bring you a limitless supply of customers.
- Know how to maximize the dollars you earn from every customer you find.
- Understand how to steadily and strategically grow your business, each and every month.

Most importantly, these methods, once in place, will continue to produce results for you without any additional work.

This is a pretty bold claim and, as Carl Sagan and Marcello Truzi said, "Extraordinary claims require extraordinary proof."

You'll find that proof in the form of clear case studies and easily reproducible experiments. What really matters to you is that you can use these ideas and will find their truth in your own experience.

As a bonus, I'll show you how to do something that I don't believe has been done before: use "predictive math" to gauge the relative likelihood of these opportunities being profitable.

Just one more thing . . .

As any father who's tried to put together a bicycle for Christmas without reading the instructions has learned, it's important to do first things first. Here's what you need to do before you dive in.

Prereading Checklist

1. *Complete all 5 steps of the short "Interactive Integration Marketing Demonstration."*

   www.IntegrationMarketing.com

   The demonstration will make the following pages more interesting and greatly enhance your understanding of the material.

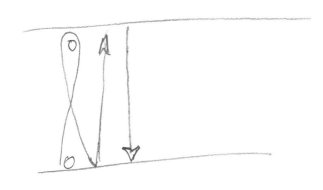

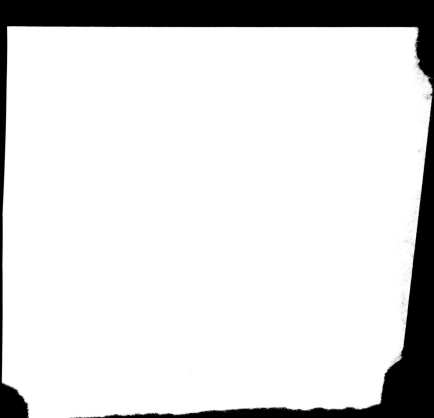

2. *Introduce yourself to the community.*

    www.IntegrationMarketing.com/dealboard

    The "Yammer Board" there is a place to hang out with other Integration Marketers. Let everyone know your name and where you're from. That board will, very shortly, become a key part of your business's growth.

Be sure to come right back and dive in. The community is fun, but we need to get started. . . .

Contents

Introduction

Why the Business World Needs Another Buzzword

This book, or at least the lead-up to it, represents something of a departure for me.

Usually, when I have the concept in mind for something I want to write, I'm like a guard dog staring at the guy who's about to hop over the fence. I can't get to it quickly enough.

I was a little more hesitant about this book. The business world is already bloated with buzzwords and trendy phrases. Adding another raises suspicion—and rightfully so. It could be perceived as the equivalent of throwing another page of self-serving "content" onto the Internet. That is: nothing more than a flowery re-wording of an existing idea.

I didn't want to be "that" guy. The guy who throws words into cyberspace simply for his own satisfaction. Or the type who rehashes the material of others for self-aggrandizement.

So, before introducing another buzzword to the business lexicon, I had to be sure of three things:

1. The concept I'm introducing has to add real value to the world. If it doesn't, I wouldn't waste my time, and I certainly wouldn't waste yours.
2. I had to be certain that Integration Marketing is indeed a phenomenon that hasn't been fully or accurately expressed before, in a way that people can use to shape their own business futures.
3. I wanted to be assured that I could present these ideas in a completely developed and practical way. Even a new idea, as shiny and appealing as it may be, is useless if it doesn't have real-world applications.

Since you're reading this, it's safe to assume that these three criteria have been met.

In the spirit of ruthless self-examination I've applied in writing this (and—with a sincere thanks to Paul Myers of www.TalkBizNews.com for his brutally honest feedback—his newsletter is one of the very few on my must-read list—it should be on yours, too), I need to be candid about what's new in this book. And, just as importantly, what's not.

You will probably recognize some of the individual tactics of Integration Marketing. Many of them are, in fact, not new at all.

This concept did not spring, fully born, from my own imagination, but rather from my observations. I kept seeing the Integration Marketing phenomenon everywhere and was constantly saying to myself, "there it is again." But, I didn't have a name to attach to it.

As these observations continued, I realized there was a significant business concept being applied in the world that had not yet been articulated in a meaningful, usable way.

So, I came up with the term "Integration Marketing" and explained it to many of the business experts I know. They hadn't heard of it either.

This led me to an interesting question. If this phenomenon already existed in the business world, but just hadn't been labeled or properly described, what's the point of naming it at all?

The phenomenon of gravity existed before Sir Isaac Newton. Without him, though, we'd be talking about that "falling from the sky thing," and we'd never be sure we were even talking about the same thing.

Newton didn't *invent* gravity. He observed it and named it. That's what I've done with Integration Marketing.

With a name comes the ability to discuss, learn, and share ideas. I want Integration Marketing to be a meme that we can share so we have a common way of talking about it and developing approaches to apply the concept in business settings.

Newton also showed us how gravity can be expressed in mathematical terms. This transformed gravity from a mysterious phenomenon to a scientific principle that could be studied, and its consequences and effects made predictable.

Can this level of rigor be applied to the world of business? I believe so. In this book, I've included a model for "predictive math" that you can use to evaluate—let's call it pretesting—the potential value of your various Integration Marketing initiatives before you actually put them into play.

Before we proceed, though, some advisories . . .

At the risk of appearing self-indulgent, the first three chapters of this book are semiautobiographical. These stories provide what I feel to be an essential context to the theories and terms and will make them far easier to understand.

One last thing before we begin. In the interests of total transparency, I'll tell you that I have an ulterior motive in writing this book, beyond wanting to make your business insanely profitable.

You'll have to wait until you read the last chapter—which itself is a great example of Integration Marketing in action—to find out my hidden motive. Jumping ahead will spoil it, though, so please don't.

Let's get started.

Integration Marketing all began (as is so often the case with science) with an observation of a common phenomenon.

As is also sometimes the case with clear observations of common phenomena, this led to the formulation of a theory with profound repercussions. These repercussions were, in fact, so profound that they not only fueled my own greatest business triumphs (and the successes of many of my students), but also (as I later came to understand) some of the greatest entrepreneurial empires in history. Microsoft, McDonald's, U.S. Steel, and even a rapper or two, just to name a few.

The first observation that warrants discussion was of a classic direct marketing ploy pointed out to me by a living business legend. This one simple trick, all by itself, could easily double your profitability, but as you'll soon see, that's only the tip of one hell of an iceberg.

Part I

The Idea

1

Digital New School Meets Profitable Old School

New School Gets Schooled ("Thank You, Sir. May I Have Another?")

I may not know you or your business, but I can tell you something about yourself that you probably don't even realize:

> You're leaving money on the table in your business. Lots of money. Right under your nose.
> You can't see it, but you will by the time you finish this book.

Let me jump into this topic by asking one of the most important business questions of the late twentieth century.

What precipitated the dot-com crash? What led so many great, innovative Internet business ideas to become commercial catastrophes?

I started writing about Internet business back in 1994 and, at the time, I felt strongly that most online businesses would ultimately fail because they lacked real *brick-and-mortar* value.

That wasn't a knock on the idea of digital enterprise. I believed that Internet-based businesses needed to observe the same kind of direct marketing discipline and fiscal common sense that successful offline businesses employed. Ultimately, the lack of those qualities is what turned the dot-com boom to bust.

Part of my own story clearly illustrates the wide-eyed ignorance of the first generation dot-commers and the desperate need for a different approach. . . .

In the 1990s, the company I was running at the time, Aesop.com, was trying to sell marketers on the value of tracking their digital advertising. The product was called "ROIbot" and it was the first remotely hosted ad tracking service on the Internet. Anyone could set up an account in seconds and begin tracking the effectiveness of online ads right away.

I thought we'd be embraced by millions overnight. I was wrong.

Yes, we had a smash opening with web business owners who already understood the importance of testing their advertising. But, the millions of customers I was expecting simply weren't knocking down my virtual door.

The company grew at a respectable pace, but not nearly as quickly as I would have liked.

I did the math and realized at that rate of growth it would take years for the business to reach any significant level of profitability.

It was the classic mistake repeated over and over by inexperienced entrepreneurs: we believed in the old adage "build a better mousetrap and the world will beat a path to your door."

This old adage just happens to be completely and utterly wrong. The number of "superior" products that fill the business graveyards proves it.

We had a fantastic product. We even had a smash opening. But these two things, while extremely helpful, are not enough to build a sustainable business.

I was crushed and frustrated.

Then, one day, we had a breakthrough that sent our growth through the roof. Here's how it happened. . . .

In addition to ad tracking, my team at Aesop had a number of other significant Internet innovations. For example, long before authors like Stephen King released their first ebooks, Aesop was at the forefront of digital publishing. In fact, Aesop was probably the first "ebook" publishing company.

Our model was clever: we simply asked print authors to allow us to digitize their existing works. It was a win-win business model. For the authors, it was a way to reach new readers with no effort on their part. For us, it was a way to instantly acquire proven products to market.

When we initially took this idea to authors, you would have thought we were selling snowplows in Tahiti. The idea of ebooks was so foreign, they couldn't see the value.

One author who wasn't resistant at all was a legendary copywriting genius by the name of Joe Sugarman. He was introduced to us by another of the early adopters of ebooks: the legendary Joe Vitale, who we also introduced to digital publishing.

Who's Joe Sugarman? You may not know the name, but you know his unparalleled contributions to direct marketing. The toll-free 800 number that customers can use to order products? That's a Joe Sugarman innovation—one of many.

And, I didn't know it at the time, but Joe provided the first mental catalyst that led to my discovery of Integration Marketing.

You've probably seen the infomercials for BluBlocker sunglasses. (Yes, that's also Joe Sugarman.) During one of our conversations, Joe told me, "Mark, you can't call us to order just a single pair of BluBlockers."

Huh? What did that mean?

He proceeded to school me on the classic direct marketing concepts of up-selling and cross-selling.

To illustrate, McDonald's provides the most fundamental lessons in these tactics. When you order a combo meal, McDonald's (before hostile documentaries and nutrition advocates—perhaps justifiably—influenced them to curtail the practice) asked, "Would you like to supersize that?"

That's an up-sell.

Order a hamburger at Mickey D's, and the person at the counter routinely asks, "would you like fries with that?"

That's a cross-sell.

It's a basic idea, but one that radically boosts profitability.

After speaking with Joe, it struck me that no one was using this technique on the Internet.

What happened whenever you went online to buy a product? You got a simple "thank you for ordering" page. No up-sell. No cross-sell. The buying experience was over, and money was left on the table (Figure 1.1).

Thank You for Your Order

Thank you for placing your order with Aesop Marketing Corporation. Your satisfaction is our main concern.

Please note that your credit card or bank statement will reflect the name **Aesop Marketing Corporation** if you ordered by credit card or checks online.

If you ordered downloadable software, you will receive an email message with downloading and/or unlocking instructions in minutes.

If you ordered products to be delivered by mail, orders are normally processed immediately upon receipt and shipped out on the first available pick-up time dependent on the method of shipment you selected. If you ordered several products to be shipped, it is possible they will arrive separately as many of our products are shipped from different physical locations. Please rest assured each will be handled as quickly as possible.

If you have any questions about your order, or wish to check the status of it, please do not hesitate to contact our <u>help desk.</u>.

Figure 1.1 Thank You for Your Order—Now Please Leave and Do Not Give Us Any More Money

It staggered me how much money many of us were leaving on the table because we hadn't employed these simple direct marketing techniques.

At Aesop we immediately started offering up-sells, cross-sells, and down-sells on our "thank-you pages." Not surprisingly, our profits took an immediate and dramatic upturn.

We knew we were on to something big. We just didn't know how big.

Figure 1.2 is an example of a particularly effective cross-sell we created for one of my earlier ebooks.

Anyone who purchased one of our business ebooks didn't get just a simple thank-you page. Instead, they'd also see a relevant offer for another of our products or services.

So, how does this tie in to the growth of ROIbot?

Two ways. The first doubled our sales immediately. The second, which you'll learn in a few moments, sent us on an exponential growth curve.

The first is probably quite obvious to you at this point: our most outrageously successful "thank-you page cross-sell" offered a free month of ROIbot. This allowed us to bring in a new steady stream of ROIbot customers from the new customers we were already generating from our ebook sales.

Thank You for Your Order

Note: Please read this message in its entirety as it contains critical **information about your order** and also shows you how to get some **free tips and tools** for maximizing your business profits and improving yourself.

You'll only see this once, so please read carefully!

Surprise Bonus. At Aesop.com, we believe in over-delivering on our promises. As a way of saying "Thank You" for your purchase, we have arranged for a discount on one of the hottest products on the net: <u>1,001 Killer Internet Marketing Tactics</u> (click this link for a pop up with info).

It normally sells for $99.90, but we have arranged for a **25% discount**—you pay only $74.90. Please click the button below to add this to your order with one click. **One click** does it!

[Collect Surprise Bonus]

Figure 1.2 Thank-You Page with Offer for "1,000 Killer Internet Marketing Tactics"

After extensive tweaking, we got to the point where 50 percent of the people who saw the offer for the free month of ROIbot would accept.

Why such an outrageously high conversion rate? In retrospect, it was simple:

1. The offer was carefully targeted toward a prequalified *warm* consumer.
2. We sold business improvement products. We already knew they were interested in boosting their profitability or they wouldn't have ordered in the first place.
3. We knew they had a credit card.
4. Perhaps the most important point of all—we knew they had just *used* the credit card, and they were confident enough in us to buy our products. The first month was free—and since they had already given us their credit card information, all they had to do was click the box to say yes.

The previous four points begin to provide insight into why Integration Marketing is so powerful, but we're still barely scratching the surface. Remember the iceberg I referred to in the Introduction? You're about to catch a glimpse of exactly how vast it is.

Still, you could walk away from this document right now, learning only what you've read to this point and vastly increase the profitability of your business.

It's true. I've seen people make that one simple adjustment—the addition of a "thank-you offer" right after someone places an order on their site — and double their revenue overnight.

But don't stop now. *We're just getting started.*

After we had played with our new "thank-you page" marketing ideas for a bit, I had a sudden insight that unlocked a method of predictable, systematic business growth for my company. But not only for Aesop, as I later realized. This idea was perhaps the single most important factor in the growth of some of the world's largest companies.

By 1999, quite a few other companies had begun following our lead in the ebook business. At the time, though, our peers were still using an antiquated order processing system that didn't take advantage of a customer's inherent willingness to do more business with them.

One day, it struck me, "Why don't we let *others* in the industry use our ROIbot up-sell on *their* thank-you pages?

We'll only pay them on commission and, for them, it will be like pulling money out of thin air.

I started doing the math and realized I had just discovered a major breakthrough for Aesop.

This idea became the single most important strategic move we ever made.

Why? What's the big deal?

Well, what's the most difficult challenge for any business? Finding qualified customers. And acquiring customers usually involves considerable time, energy, money, or likely, all three.

With this new strategy, we could generate a steady stream of new customers on a regular basis—all from just a single conversation with one other company.

All we had to do was keep finding these deals and our company would steadily grow—with little time, energy, or money involved.

Think carefully about that. This concept can literally mean millions for you if you do.

I feel compelled to make certain you don't walk away from this book without truly grasping the power of this idea.

It is so important, in fact, that I'm going to underscore it with a short chapter of its own, using a lesson from someone who is closer to being a real-life Yoda than anyone I've ever met.

Your business Jedi training begins now.

2

A Real-Life Yoda on Billion Dollar Businesses

Thinking big is not as easy as it sounds.

Sure, you may be able to make your business work at a relatively low volume, but how do you ratchet it up so that you're doing more business, with more customers, and enjoying the kind of large-scale success you know you're capable of?

Many people talk about that, but how many actually *do* it?

Will you be one of them?

Reading this book has started you on the path. As you'll soon learn, Integration Marketing provides a clear methodology for elevating the scale of any business, doing so in a very low-risk, predictable fashion.

But before we get into the specifics, it will be instructive to take a moment to understand why this is so profoundly important.

Here's a little story that should make it abundantly clear.

In learning how to think big, I picked up some of the most important lessons in my life from an organization that only knows how to do things in a big way—the U.S. Army.

When I was in U.S. Army Officer Candidate School in Fort Benning, Georgia, one of our instructors was the closest thing to an honest-to-goodness Jedi Master of anyone I've ever met.

We called him Yoda. But not to his face.

Most of the classes at OCS took place in a massive concrete cube called Building 4. To the students, it was "Building Snore," because lessons were not exactly, shall we say, stimulating.

Surviving Building Snore is a rite of passage among officer candidates. General Colin Powell took classes there. So did the Panamanian dictator Manuel

Noriega, who would later be deposed by Powell's American military.

We used to joke that the Pentagon was testing a new weapon on the building—antifun rays. That had to be the case because even the most potentially interesting lecture would be drained of all vitality before it was served to the students.

So, there I was, sitting at my desk in Building Snore, prepared to enter a comalike state. Imagine my surprise when Yoda walked in.

WHAP!

He slapped a massive book on the desk, startling more than a few sleeping students.

"Front ... Leaning ... Rest," he hissed.

That's Army-speak for "get into position to do push-ups." It's what you hear from drill sergeants, not lecturers on military theory.

In just those few seconds, it became clear we weren't in Building Snore anymore. We were in a place where warriors were trained.

After our short "rest" in the front leaning position, Yoda began his lecture with a very simple question, "What is the one skill that defines a leader?"

One candidate blurted out, "Sir, communication skills."

Yoda smirked. "Oh, really?" he said. "So, let's say you have a suicidal tactical approach and you communicate it oh so clearly to your troops. This makes you a leader?"

"Charisma!" another blurted out.

"What?! Yoooou must be joking! So, you're a tactical moron but, by golly, you look good in your BDUs. I just wrote your tombstone for you. No charge. Next!"

This increasingly painful back-and-forth went on for about 10 minutes before everyone gave up.

"No one?" Yoda asked, with a combination of pity and scorn in his voice. "Not a single one of you has the first clue about leadership?"

(In retrospect, this exercise may have seemed cruel, but it was very, very necessary. Most of the candidates in that classroom were former enlisted soldiers and non-commissioned officers. We were supposed to be the "best of the best" from our respective units. We were full of ourselves, and it showed.

Yoda opened our eyes to the fact that we were in no way ready to lead men into combat.

This, by the way, is the same attitude I see in so many business owners. Some enjoy a little success and think they're ready to move up to the next level. The sad fact is they're simply not prepared.)

Oh, so what was the correct answer to Yoda's question?

He taught us that the single defining quality a leader must have, above all others, is the ability to . . .

See the battlefield.

Read that again.

Put that on a sticky note. Post it on your computer monitor and your bathroom mirror.

Heck, tattoo it on your eyelids if it means you'll never forget those words.

See the battlefield.

This is one of those rare bits of knowledge that is so profound and important that you can say those words to yourself three times a day, every single day, and you wouldn't be overdoing it.

See the battlefield.

Even though none of us could think of the right answer when Yoda asked the question, isn't it obvious? You can be incredibly charismatic. You can be a brilliant tactician. You can communicate with crystal clarity.

But you are doomed if you don't see the battlefield—if you don't understand what is happening on the terrain around you.

So, it's easy, right? Just open your eyes and see the business battlefield laid out before you, and everything will come up roses with flowers of gold, ripe for the picking.

Not so fast, my eager apprentice.

Looking at something is not the same as "seeing" it. You must be able to understand, evaluate, and make decisions based on what you see. That's what seeing truly means.

There's a way to reach this level of seeing, to make the battlefield become more clearly defined. It involves a word that I hesitate to put on paper right now.

I hesitate because it's a word that gets bandied about ad nauseam in business circles, but is rarely used meaningfully. It's the kind of buzzword that business people toss around to give their message greater meaning and gravitas, even though their poor understanding of the word's true definition makes it little more than a verbal fashion accessory.

The word is—*strategy.*

Okay, stop right there.

Do yourself a favor and forget every single thing you've ever heard about the word "strategy." Most of what you've heard comes from the University of Greater Buzzwords and has all the legitimacy of a Caribbean medical degree.

I'm going to give you my own definition of strategy. It's one that you won't find in any textbook, and you certainly won't hear it from any of the so-called business gurus. This is something I've developed from years of study, military training, and hands-on business experience.

Ready?

> **Strategy:** A conceptual approach for achieving an aim that allows you to see the battlefield (no matter how complex it becomes) and make consistently effective decisions quickly (even when a correct move is seemingly impossible to find), *no matter what may arise.*

Put another way: when you're tired, when your enemy's moves are baffling, when nothing makes sense—you go back to your strategy and it provides the answer to "what do we do now?"

If your strategy is a good one, the answer to that question will tend to push you in the right direction.

If you don't have a strategy, or if your strategy is poor, your actions will tend to push you further and further in the wrong direction.

Most people equate strategy with planning. They are not the same thing.

We can plan stuff until the cows come home, and the best of us will only be able to concoct a handful of plans to anticipate a variety of scenarios.

But to what end?

The fact is, we *cannot* anticipate every eventuality in life or in business.

We *cannot* predict with anything approaching 100 percent certainty what might occur in the future. Therefore, we need a *strategy* that allows us to tackle situations as they arise and move through them regardless of their nature, so that they don't disrupt our efforts to achieve our aims.

Now, this may seem antithetical to the notion of "seeing the battlefield." Isn't seeing the battlefield the primary skill of a leader? Isn't it the case that if you could see the battlefield perfectly you would not need the help of a strategy to make the right decision?

Well yes—if we were superbeings with omniscient knowledge and infinite intelligence. But we're not.

By definition, humans are always making decisions based on limited information. The human eye takes in about a gigabit of raw data per second—and only a small fraction of that is processed in conscious memory.

So, seeing the battlefield is not so much a matter of perfect vision, but of selection.

With a well-formed strategy, you can more easily select information that is relevant to your aim—and then you are more likely to make decisions based on information that is more likely to help you achieve those aims.

So, how does all this fit into business?

As you'll learn in upcoming pages, Integration Marketing provides you a way of truly seeing the battlefield and a clear method of developing a genuine well-formed strategy to turn your business into a profit monster.

You're about to learn how to do just that.

As Clausewitz's student von Moltke said, "*No battle plan survives contact with the enemy.*"

A plan is rigid. A strategy is fluid.

In the simplest terms possible: we need to have things to do that constantly bring us closer to our objectives. If your strategy does not provide a framework that allows you to make sense out of chaos and a guiding principle for real decisions and actions on the ground, then it is a poor strategy.

Strike that. It's not a strategy at all. It's a recipe for doom.

Integration Marketing, ultimately, provides us with a powerful strategy. A real one. One that will let you score the business equivalent of game-winning touchdowns when and as needed.

If this seems like a simple idea, well it is.

It's a simple idea that explains the historic successes of Microsoft, McDonald's, and U.S. Steel, not to mention bringing greater success to my own companies than we ever dreamed possible.

In fact, a good strategy has to be simple. It needs to be something you can remember and communicate when the bullets are flying.

First, though, it might be useful to give you a taste of just how powerful Integration Marketing can be.

This simple idea has built business mega-empires and shaped entire industries. You're about to learn about two of them . . .

If you think you know where I'm going with this, I'll caution you to pay close attention.

That up-selling and cross-selling McDonald's does, that I mentioned earlier in the book? Believe it or not, that's *not* McDonald's big Integration Marketing triumph. Important Integration Marketing tactics, yes. Approaches that made the company a lot of money, sure. But, compared to what you are about to learn, supersizing and extra french fries are child's play.

McDonald's big Integration Marketing play was one of massive strategic importance.

And then there's the story of how an unknown computer geek used the *concepts you've just learned* to become a billionaire.

3

How Integration Marketing Transformed a Self-Confessed Geek into One of History's Most Influential People

I have long maintained that Microsoft's Earth-conquering success is due much more to its incredible (yet often extremely subtle) marketing prowess than to the quality of its products. You're about to find out the degree to which that's true, and it's a story that will make you a true believer in the potency of Integration Marketing.

But, first, let's do a minirecap of what we've covered so far.

We've discussed successes with simple integrations: integrating additional offers into our own offers and our offers into the offers of others. From these activities, I formulated a simple definition of Integration Marketing.

Integration Marketing (early simplified definition):
The integration of one marketing process into another.

Now, this is good as far as it goes. It's incomplete, though. It reveals a very important piece of the picture, but there's still much more behind the curtain. (What you'll learn in the next chapter is far more powerful, but we're not quite ready for that yet.)

And, as long as we're dealing in definitions, let's address some common misconceptions that have popped up since I began teaching these concepts:

- *"Integrated Marketing Communications" is NOT the same as Integration Marketing.* The two are totally different. Integrated Marketing Communications (IMC) is a concept commonly taught in universities. Integration Marketing isn't. IMC is all about ensuring that your marketing message is consistent across various media. Not to minimize the importance of doing this, but it's a completely different animal than Integration Marketing.

- *Up-sells, cross-sells, down-sells, and the like are NOT the same as Integration Marketing.* These are individual tactics that have also been around for years. They are important subsets of Integration Marketing, but not the be-all, end-all that defines the concept. To say that "Integration Marketing is cross-selling" completely misses the big picture and cuts off options that are outrageously profitable. They are but a few of the infinite Integration Marketing possibilities, as you'll soon see.

I finally started teaching Integration Marketing concepts to the general public around 2002, using the earlier definition, but the concepts have evolved significantly since that time.

There is an expanded definition. It's wordier, but it's more accurate. It's a good idea, though, to get your head around the simplified definition first, because it's easier to understand and can enable you to hit the ground running right away.

Now, onto the stories that will show you even more vividly how to see the battlefield and enable us to discuss an even broader and, ultimately, more useful definition of Integration Marketing.

Bill Gates and the Meeting That Changed the World

The younger Bill Gates may not have looked like a business cutthroat, but history shows the kind of cojones he had right from the beginning as he transformed Microsoft into one of the world's most well-known brand names.

Some people call the meeting between Microsoft and IBM executives, in which Microsoft sold DOS to IBM, the most significant meeting in the history of business.

It was, but not for the reasons experts think.

That meeting provides lessons in being bold (Microsoft didn't even own DOS—all Gates had was a possible deal to purchase it), minimizing your personal risk, and leveraging the assets of others. These are enviable qualities, but they are thin soup compared to the *real* lessons that emerged from that meeting.

The importance of the Microsoft-IBM conversation lies in the deal points Gates negotiated:

- Microsoft had the right to sell upgrades of MS-DOS to end users.
- Microsoft had the right to sell MS-DOS to other computer manufacturers.

Observers didn't realize it at the time, but this deal demonstrated that Microsoft understood, on a very deep level, exactly what would drive company growth: Integration Marketing.

Let's dissect the deal and understand the real strategy of Bill Gates.

First, notice that Microsoft acquired customers *without having to sell anything*. DOS was integrated into the sale of the computer. IBM's customers became Microsoft's customers.

That shrewd move alone would have made Gates a multimillionaire. It was the deal points, though, that made him the richest man in the world.

Adding the rights to sell upgrades to end users was critical. By signing this deal, IBM essentially turned over all of its customers to Microsoft. Since Microsoft had the right to sell upgrades, they could ask computer-buying customers to register for those upgrades. Word of mouth about DOS upgrades was extremely high among computer users, so there was considerable pressure to do so.

Witness the genius of what Microsoft negotiated. Not only did they get a sale served up to them on IBM's own silver platters, but also they acquired a full customer relationship along with it.

And that relationship was deeper than IBM anticipated, deeper even than IBM's connections with its own customer base.

Look at the comparative visibility of built-in brand advertising. The IBM logo was on the computer chassis, which is essentially a piece of furniture. But the computer user's eyes are on the screen, and they are told every time they boot up the computer that they're running a Microsoft operating system.

Quick Quiz

1. Who manufactured your current computer? What about your first one?

If the answer is not "Apple," most people don't know the answer.

2. What's your operating system?

It's a rare person that doesn't know whether his or her computer runs Mac, Windows, or Linux.

Furthermore, by negotiating the right to make this same deal with other companies, Gates set the stage for an extraordinary Integration Marketing strategy. He wanted to position himself, whenever a new computer was manufactured, to be the operating system of choice by having his software preinstalled on that machine.

They don't use the term Integration Marketing in Redmond, but it's clear that the minds behind Microsoft understand its power. It's seen in the integration of Internet Explorer as a primary strategy to achieve Internet dominance, and it's seen, as well, in Microsoft's exclusion of Java to fend off SUN Microsystems' own Integration Marketing efforts.

Now you know how one of the world's great business empires was built. Not by word of mouth, not by exceptional products (no disrespect—this isn't an anti-Microsoft screed), but through Integration Marketing.

Later, I made another observation that led to a more fully developed definition of Integration Marketing—one that would open up even more possibilities.

McDonald's and "Location, Location, Location"

As we've discussed, you learn a great deal about McDonald's basic Integration Marketing tactics as soon as you step up to the counter. When you're asked if you want fries with your order, you're seeing a live demonstration of old school marketing that can be categorized as an Integration Marketing tactic.

But what's really important at McDonald's is what happens long before the first Big Mac is assembled.

Robert Kiyosaki tells a terrific story about Ray Kroc, the founder of McDonald's. Kroc asked a room full of MBAs, "What business is McDonald's in?"

Of course, they answered "the hamburger business." He immediately corrected them.

"Ladies and gentlemen, I am not in the hamburger business. I'm in real estate."

What the heck did he mean by *that*?

You're probably thinking that he's referring to the property value of the thousands upon thousands of restaurants owned by McDonald's, aren't you? Yes, McDonald's has locations in 118 countries, and the collective value of those properties must be astronomical.

But that's not it. McDonald's doesn't sell those properties. It's in the business of flipping burgers, not real estate.

When Kroc talked about real estate, he was referring to the inherent *marketing* value of every location at which McDonald's plants its Golden Arches.

McDonald's looks for flows of potential traffic and then integrates its stores right smack dab into the middle of that flow.

The company finds out where people are likely to be hungry and hurried, and locates their stores in the midst of that marketing hotbed.

Think of where you see McDonald's—shopping malls, city centers, highway rest stops.

This is what we mean by seeing the battlefield. McDonald's has read its battlefield to a tee and now dominates it.

As you'll learn in a moment, in Chapter 4's "Language of Integration Marketing," McDonald's is simply looking for Integration Points as a strategic guiding principle.

The company that Ray Kroc built is now playing with other stealthy "Reverse Integration Marketing" ploys. For example, it is integrating the placement of "McCafe" coffee shops in existing stores to increase profitability.

Starbucks sees this as a legitimate threat to its latte dominance as well it should.

With the Microsoft and McDonald's examples planted firmly in mind, this is probably a good time to introduce the better, more refined definition of Integration Marketing.

> **Integration Marketing (newer, more complete, definition):** The integration of a Unit of Marketing Value (a brand message, an offer, a sale, a store—anything that adds marketing impact to your business) into an existing Integration Point (inside a Traffic or Transaction Stream).

If that doesn't make immediate sense to you, don't worry. It will become even clearer very soon.

Using Integration Marketing as a strategic way of thinking allows you to find opportunities that would have been otherwise invisible and to find opportunities with significantly lower risk.

In the section about Strategic Integration Marketing, I'm going to tell you why this is not only important, but may soon be the most significant thing you've done since the day you launched your business.

That's a bold statement, but, as you'll see in a moment, it is absolutely true.

To fully understand the definition you just read—I owe it to you to translate some of the lingo I inserted in there. What follows is the basic "Language of Integration." You'll want to master this so you can "do" Integration Marketing quickly and easily, both inside and outside your organization.

There are times when the right word makes the unseen seen. Knowing these words will allow you to more clearly *see* the invisible opportunities all around you on your own business battlefield.

After that, I'll give you a very simple method for invigorating your business with a lethal Integration Marketing strategy.

4

Talking the Business Growth Talk

The Language of Integration Marketing (Part 1)

If you're a little on the impatient side (I freely plead guilty to that flaw myself), you might feel the urge to skip forward past the boring definitions and get to the *real* action.

Don't make that mistake. To succeed in Integration Marketing, definitions are *critical* to the action.

As you absorb the terminology in this section, you're going to achieve a couple of important things. First, you'll acquire a language with which to discuss your newly acquired profit-making powers with current and future partners.

The Building Snore Yoda said that communication may not be as important as seeing the battlefield, but without it, you'll be fighting your battles on your own. It's much easier with an army.

And, second, these definitions will act as launch points to stimulate your thinking.

I strongly recommend that you get your head around these terms before diving into "The Language of Integration Marketing (Part 2)," which you'll find in Chapter 7.

It might take you a few minutes to get a good feel for these definitions. Read them and let them sink in for a moment. Take your time.

This small investment of time will pay you huge dividends. Once you master these terms, you'll start seeing potential Integration Points everywhere. You'll have a shared language you can use with your potential Integration Marketing Partners to strike Integration Marketing Deals.

In that paragraph you just read, there are three new terms alone that are begging to be defined.

So, let's dive right in.

Remember how we initially defined Integration Marketing?

Integration Marketing[1] (early simplified definition): The integration of one marketing process into another.

Now, let's spin that off and create meaning for the terms you just learned:

Integration Marketing Deals: An agreement between two or more parties that uses Integration Marketing tactics. As with any legitimate deal, it should clearly outline how both parties will benefit, as well as their respective responsibilities.
Integration Marketing Partners: Those with whom you do Integration Marketing Deals.

That's a start, but let's ramp up these definitions a little.

Unit of Marketing Value (UMV):. It's what you integrate. It can be an offer (for a sale or a freebie, something that serves as a lead-in), a branding message, a new marketing process, or a sale, etc. It must be something that provides

(continued)

a specific marketing benefit to the integrator (see next)—and ideally—also to the owner of the Integration Point (see later).

Integrator: The party in an Integration Marketing Deal who provides the UMV.

Traffic Stream: Any place where people are gathering—in a store; at a particular physical location; or even a virtual locale, like a web site or a blog.

Transaction Stream: The point at which exchanges or transactions regularly occur between merchants and their customers. It is important to note that a Transaction Stream only becomes visible once a transaction—any transaction—is taking place.

(This doesn't necessarily have to be a monetary transaction. It can include transactions in which information or data are traded—such as a sign-up process where contact details are exchanged for access to a freebie, like an ebook.)

Integration Point: The point inside a Traffic or Transaction Stream at which you can insert a UMV.

And, now, with these definitions in play, let's reintroduce our expanded definition of Integrated Marketing, which will now have greater meaning for you.

Now, if you're like me, definitions become more real when you make them three-dimensional. In other words, when you can see them in real-world situations.

> **Integration Marketing[2] (newer, more accurate, definition):** The integration of a UMV (a brand message, an offer, a sale, a store—anything that adds marketing impact to your business) into an existing Integration Point (inside a Traffic or Transaction Stream).

So, let's do that, using an example from earlier in the book.

Remember how Aesop asked other companies to put the ROIbot cross-sell on their thank-you pages?

We identified many companies that had unused real estate in their online sales processes. They were selling products related to ours, but up-selling nothing.

Here's how this particular Integration Marketing Deal can be broken down using the terminology in this section:

The Integration Point: The point in the other companies' transaction streams right after the sale—the "thank you for ordering" page.

The Unit of Marketing Value: The proven cross-sell page that effectively sold people on our ROIbot service.

The Integrator: That was yours truly. We provided the UMV for the owner of the Integration Point to insert into his Transaction Stream.

The Integration Marketing Deal: Here's where you can see the win-win nature of a great Integration Marketing Deal. We contacted companies and told them that all they had to do was put our customized ROIbot cross-sell page in place of their existing thank-you page. We would pay them a monthly recurring commission on the customers they generated for us. Their existing thank-you page was generating no income for them and was simply a wasted opportunity. With our deal, there was minimal effort on their part in exchange for a continuous revenue stream from Aesop. For Aesop, we considerably expanded our customer base without investing significant time or money.

This should stimulate your thinking processes on how you can construct similar deals for your company.

But we still have some important miles to travel on this road, and there are many types of Integration Points and Integration Marketing Deals to discuss.

Before we talk about more sophisticated deals, though, let's spend a little time on how to use these ideas in a practical and deliberate way for your company.

It's all about these "three little words" that every business owner loves to hear.

Part II

The Strategy

5

Why Strategic Integration Marketing?

Three Magic Words

As you begin the process of considering possible Integration Marketing Deals, it's critical that you keep these three little words at the center of your thinking:

More. Profit. Faster.

As I explained earlier, a business strategy, at its best, will provide you with a guideline that allows you to make better decisions, faster.

But what's a *better* decision?

What is the kind of decision that will render measurably greater profits?

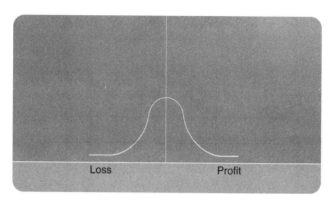

Figure 5.1   Total Number of Business Deals: Negative ROI Deals on the Left, Positive ROI Deals on the Right

Integration Marketing is a strategic way of thinking that allows you to find opportunities that would have been otherwise invisible, and to find opportunities with significantly lower risk.

Putting these words into action may be the most important thing you do in your business.

But let's take those words and look at them visually.

Imagine the bell curve in Figure 5.1 represents the total number of business deals you can make ranging from those that render a loss to those that render a profit.

Once you master the concept of Integration Marketing, you will be able to quickly recognize Integration Marketing opportunities, thereby radically increasing the number of doors you can open to grow your business.

It's all about seeing the battlefield.

For example, if you're an NFL quarterback without any concept of how to run your team's offense, the action taking place on the field will make no sense to you.

Understand the intricacies of that offense, and you suddenly begin seeing open receivers and scoring opportunities.

In the language of business: you'll not only see limitless ways of bringing in new customers, but you'll also find countless new avenues for increasing the profitability of your existing business (Figure 5.2).

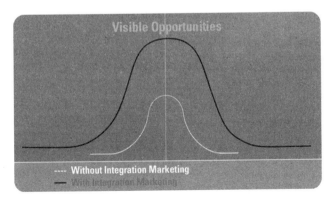

Figure 5.2 Integration Marketing Creates More Visible Opportunities

As you see, with an understanding of Integration Marketing, you can actually *see* more opportunity in the business world.

So why does it matter so much to have *more* Integration Marketing opportunities?

Integration Marketing is usually, by definition, low risk, low investment, and high return. If you act on a significant number of opportunities with a high upside and minimal risk, your business is going to expand.

But let's play devil's advocate here. Let's imagine that there are an equal number of good and bad Integration Marketing opportunities. If that is genuinely the case, your diagram of opportunities would look like Figure 5.3.

(Let me note here that defining a bad business opportunity involves more than just sheer monetary terms. After all, if an opportunity costs you a $10 investment and earns you $11, it may look good on the surface. But what if it also costs you considerable time and energy? That takes the luster off your $1 profit by absorbing time and energy that you could be using to generate additional money in different, potentially more profitable deals.)

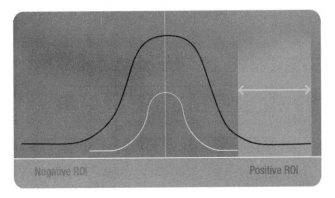

Negative ROI   Positive ROI

Figure 5.3 Highlight Shows New Profitable Deals Revealed by Integration Marketing

In reality, the diagram above is flawed. If you really want to create a visual that shows the potential of Integration Marketing opportunities, it would look like Figure 5.4.

The "universe" of Integration Marketing opportunities is a more profitable one than the average. How so?

Integration Marketing exploits are, by design, likely to have a much higher return on investment (ROI) than others.

The time, energy, and money you need to invest in an Integration Marketing Deal will, by definition, be

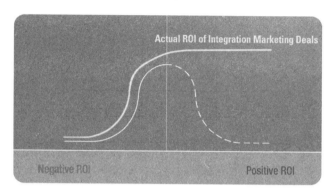

Figure 5.4   Since Integration Marketing Deals Are More Likely to Have a High ROI, Your "Universe" of High Profit Deals is Much Higher

lower than other forms of marketing. Therefore, even if returns are low, you're getting a return for a very small investment. Further, the returns tend to be residual.

Almost every Integration Marketing Deal I've ever struck required *no cash investment* whatsoever. And, once I established an infrastructure for reproducing the deal, each new spin-off of that original deal required only an e-mail or phone call to set up.

You create it. Then, you can forget about it and work on other deals while your new customers and new profits start adding up.

Remember, since the profits tend to be residual, a growing collection of small payoff deals can grow from a trickle to a mighty river over time.

That doesn't mean that there is *zero* risk involved.

The majority of Integration Marketing Deals will work extremely well for you. But not all.

Without knowing which deal is more profitable, it's conceivable that you could pick one that will actually generate a net loss in time, energy, or money.

And the more opportunities you generate, the more likely it is that you'll stumble on one or two that have a potentially negative ROI.

Don't let that prospect intimidate you. Business is inherently about risk. Integration Marketing lowers that risk substantially.

Can we lower it even more?

Remember when I said it's possible to predict with great accuracy which Integration Marketing opportunities will work? In upcoming pages, I'll show you the Integration Marketing Scoring System. With that system in place, you'll be assured that you're more consistently choosing deals in the upper ranges of potential ROI.

In English?

More. Profit. Faster.

Do Integration Marketing—do it right and do it often—and those three words will become your personal business mantra.

Now you may be thinking, "all of this sounds wonderful, but how do we make it happen in the real world?"

Great question. Turn the page . . .

6

Taking That First Step Forward

*Creating Your Integration Marketing
Growth Strategy*

Okay, let's move from ideas to action.

How do you actually turn everything we've covered so far into a workable marketing strategy that you can use to guide your organization to a more profitable level?

Using the concepts we've discussed so far, it's not as hard as you might think.

And you'll be surprised by how much fun you'll have doing it.

Four Step Integration Marketing Growth Strategy

1. *Identify potential Integration Marketing Deals.* For example, create a cross-sell offer for one of your

products that e-newsletter publishers can offer on their thank-you pages.

2. *Conduct proof of concept testing.* Test the UMV you intend to integrate. Make sure it's having the desired effect.

3. *Strike your first deal.* Remember, great Integration Marketing Deals should involve minimal time, energy, and money on your part.

If you did step 2 properly, the deal will be profitable for the owner of the Integration Point, and thus an easy sell.

4. *Duplicate and scale.* If you do it once, you don't stop there. You do it again. And again.

And again.

Great businesses understand the value of replication. If a simple action works and generates profits, you keep on repeating it.

It's not a complicated strategy, but some of the most effective strategies in business history have been the simplest, most obvious ones.

Why do many businesses fail? Because they feel compelled to keep on trying different approaches instead of simply scaling what already works.

Don't do that.

Instead, build your business around what I call "Scalable Marketing Processes." This means, instead of reinventing the wheel with your marketing each time, you find a method that works and you scale it up. You don't find a new method—you just use the same method more often. Integration Marketing Deals are not only low risk/high profit but almost always extremely scalable.

You'll also want to constantly develop and improve "Internal Integration Marketing" (see the next chapter) to increase the profit you earn per customer. Meanwhile, the plan above will create the continuing flow of new customers that is the lifeblood of any growing business.

As you identify, pursue, and develop Integration Marketing Deals, how do you ensure that you're using your company's resources most efficiently?

You have to ask yourself....

Do You Need an Integration Marketing Czar?

I would strongly recommend you designate someone as your Integration Marketing Czar. (You could use a prosaic title like Director or Coordinator, but an approach as innovative as Integration Marketing warrants a much more eye-opening job title.)

This individual's responsibility will be to identify and exploit specific types of Integration Marketing Deals.

Note that I said "identify" and "exploit." I did not say "invent."

As I mentioned earlier, many companies innovate themselves right out of existence. They put creativity ahead of profitability and feel the need to generate new marketing ideas, even if they have a quiver full of arrows that are already consistently hitting the target.

It's usually more profitable to identify particular types of Integration Marketing Deals that work for your company and then duplicate and scale, duplicate and scale, and duplicate and scale. This is the mandate you hand your Integration Marketing Czar.

Duplicate and scale. Keep repeating the process for as long as it works.

One of my students has a person in his company assigned to the task of finding the exact type of Integration Marketing Deal that we used to build ROI-bot. He finds web sites with underutilized real estate and makes deals to integrate his company's selling message.

Every day, he goes out and finds companies with whom he can integrate various offers.

Since he knows exactly what kind of partner he's seeking, and exactly what kind of deal he wants to make, neither he (nor his company) spend valuable time formulating grandiose plans that may or may not ever come to fruition.

If a potential Integration Marketing Deal comes across your desk and it doesn't fit the strategy you've outlined, you should almost always reject it.

Yes, there are exceptions. Ask yourself:

- Will it be easy? (I mean *really* easy.)
- Will it support our brand strategy? (That is, does it allow you to be who you are?)
- Does it fit in with our values? (Would you be proud if your grandkids and your customers found out about it?)

Only if you can answer "yes" to all of these questions should you consider it, and even then proceed with caution.

Increasing profits with minimal investment of time and energy. It's not a fancy idea, but it sure does make a lot of sense, doesn't it?

Makes a lot of dollars, too.

Now, let's open up new worlds of possibility for your business. The new terms you'll learn in the next chapter will do just that.

Part III

The Mastery

7

More Words that Matter

The Language of Integration Marketing (Part 2)

Yes, we're going to throw some more definitions at you.

"But Mark," you may be grumbling, "why are you waiting until this far into the book to define essential terminology?"

For the same reason that a runner doesn't burst into a sprint without warming up first.

If you had read the following definitions earlier, the overload of information may have shut down your interest and attention. You might have been turned off without having the chance to realize the full potential of Integration Marketing.

These definitions—and the scoring system you'll learn in the following chapter—will give you a deeper understanding of Integration Marketing as a strategic discipline.

More to the point, you're about to gain some serious firepower that you can use to generate fresh, new, *effective* ideas.

Let's start by recalling the types of *Integration Points*.

Remember that an Integration Point is the point at which you can insert a UMV.

There are two types of Integration Points: those that occur along Traffic Streams and those that occur along Transaction Streams.

A Traffic Stream is any place where people are gathering (recall how McDonald's locates restaurants at places where there are likely to be large numbers of hungry people). A *Traffic Stream Integration Point* exists anywhere people are passing by without conducting a transaction.

A Transaction Stream refers to the point at which a transaction with a person is taking place. A *Transaction Stream Integration Point* exists only when a transaction is actually occurring.

Let's clarify the difference. If you integrate something into a storefront, but it's only on display, the integration is a Traffic Stream Integration Point. It's there to appeal to the flow of potential customers.

On the other hand, if this item of value is at the checkout counter, or if it's a verbal up-sell from a cashier as the initial purchase is being made, it's a Transaction Stream Integration Point.

Types of Traffic Streams
- Advertising
- Geographic
- Storefront

There are others, but these should get you thinking.

Types of Transaction Streams
- Lead generation
- Post sale
- Bundled sale

Again, there are others, but these will get you thinking.

Transaction Stream Integration Points are more valuable.

Why? Well, it's as simple as the difference between cool and warm.

The person who is involved in a transaction has already demonstrated important qualifications—an interest in your products, a willingness to purchase from you, and available cash or a viable credit card.

To drive this point home even further, let's look at Figure 7.1.

In general, higher value Integration Points will have fewer people looking at them.

This makes great sense if you think about it. A thousand people might walk past a storefront, but the

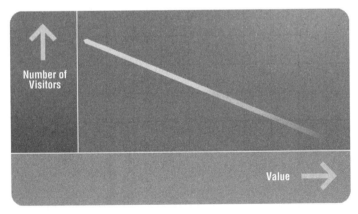

Figure 7.1   Value versus Number of Visitors

50 people who walk in to buy something are the ones most likely to bring value to your business.

Here's one of the differences between successful marketers and inexperienced rookies. The rookie will take the "sucker's bet" marketing move every time. They'll go for high traffic with low value because they think, usually erroneously, that high traffic will result in more customers.

It's the siren allure of large numbers. And, as was the case with sailors in mythology, that siren call will send you crashing into the rocks more times than not.

Figure 7.2 provides another way of looking at it that explains the point even more clearly.

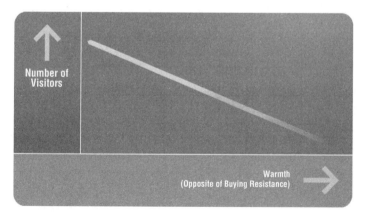

Figure 7.2   Warmth versus Number of Visitors

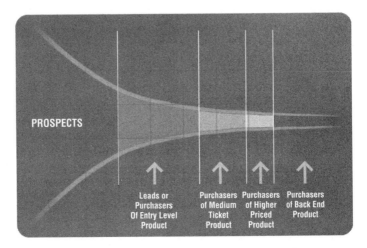

Figure 7.3 Typical Marketing Funnel

As you move toward Integration Points in which you interact with fewer people, the overall warmth of those prospects tends to increase.

To look at it another way, let's analyze a typical marketing funnel (Figure 7.3).

The further along the marketing funnel you travel with your UMV, the more effectiveness you gain because the customer is more committed to the sales process.

Here are some more essential Integration Marketing definitions.

Internal Integration Marketing: This happens when the UMV and the Integration Point are owned by the same entity.

Envision using a "thank you for purchasing" page on one of your web sites to sell yet another of your products. Or, imagine McDonald's asking you if you want some fries with that burger you just bought. Those are but two of the limitless ways this can occur.

External Integration Marketing: This happens when a UMV owned by one business entity is inserted into an Integration Point owned by another business entity.

Our ROIbot integration deal is a perfect example. Microsoft bundling the sale of DOS with IBM computers is another. McDonald's up-selling Cokes is another still. Again, these are but three ships in a sea of infinite possibility.

These two definitions are extremely important.

You can use Internal Integration Marketing to improve word of mouth about your business and increase the profitability of your own marketing processes.

This is extremely important. With these methods you can turn a $100 transaction into a $1,000 transaction. You can turn customers into evangelists.

Those are wonderful things, but it's External Integration Marketing where the real cash fireworks go off.

External Integration Marketing results in the business miracle of exponentially increasing your number of customers. This is where the bulk of your Integration Marketing energy should be focused.

> **Integration Marketing Score:** A mathematical method for predicting the potential value of an Integration Marketing Deal.

Here are a couple more definitions you need to absorb.

This is explained in detail in the next chapter.

> **Integration Marketing Factor:** The rate of speed at which an Integration Marketing Deal will provide value (measured in sales, leads, or exposure) to your company. To find the Integration Marketing Factor, you simply do the following math:
>
> Integration Point Factor × Target Factor
>
> = Integration Marketing Factor

Okay, maybe that's not so easy to understand—yet. My point is that we've invented mathematical formulas you can use as predictive tools for determining the best Integration Marketing Deals for your business.

This is like having your own financial crystal ball.

Your instruction manual for using that crystal ball is in the next chapter.

8

Minimizing Guesswork, Maximizing Growth

Using the Integration Marketing Score

Wouldn't it be a perfect world if you absorbed the lessons of Integration Marketing and found yourself with several potential deals in front of you and an unlimited amount of time to pick the best ones?

Let's face facts. We don't live in a perfect world.

If you want to achieve those magic words—More Profit Faster—you're going to want to choose the Integration Marketing Deals that are most likely to become outrageously profitable.

What if you could, with astounding consistency, predict which potential Integration Marketing Deals are in the highlighted section of the curve?

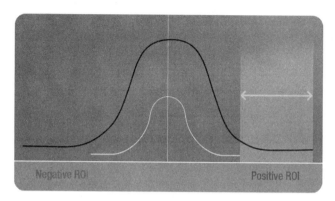

Negative ROI   Positive ROI

Figure 8.1   The Universe of Integration Marketing Deals

It's time for you to meet the *Integration Marketing Score*.

As far as I know, this is the first time anyone has ever attempted to apply predictive math to a marketing method. We're moving into uncharted waters here and, in a sense, creating the rules as we go.

But, essentially, that's what the original mathematicians did when they developed laws that said numbers will behave in a certain way.

Along those same lines, we're going to define the rules for calculating Integration Marketing potential. These rules won't have any practical usefulness in any other field of mathematics, but you don't care about that.

What you want to know is: *which deals are most likely to render the highest ROI?*

The Integration Marketing Score will do that for you.

To help explain how this system works, let's set some rules, beginning with the fact that we will use the number "1" as a base.

Things that have a *positive* impact on your marketing will have a value *higher* than "1."

Things that have *no* impact, one way or another, have a value of exactly "1."

Things that have a *negative* impact on your marketing will have a value *greater than zero and less than* "1."

(There are no negative numbers, or even a zero, in this system.)

As you play with the numbers, all of this will make more sense to you.

Step 1: Find Your Integration Marketing Factor

Remember in the previous chapter, we said you would need to find your Integration Marketing Factor. You do so by multiplying the following:

Integration Point Factor × Target Factor = Integration Marketing Factor

Let's start by assigning a numerical value to your Integration Point Factor, be it a Traffic Stream Integration Point or a Transaction Stream Integration Point:

Traffic Stream Integration Points	
Advertising Integration (no call to action)	0.01
Advertising Integration (with call to action)	0.05
Web page Integration (outside of a transaction)	0.1
Geographic Integration	0.5
Transaction Stream Integration Points	
Postsale bundled advertising	0.75
Postlead generator Integration	1.0
Postsale Integration (customer data not transmitted)	2.0
Bundled sale Integration (customer data not transmitted)	3.0
Postsale Integration (customer data transmitted)	4.0
Bundled sale Integration (customer data transmitted)	6.0

Now, let's select our Target Factor from these pre-defined values:

Target Factors	
Different target market and no likely crossover	0.5
Different target market, but likely partial crossover (in demographics or psychographics)	0.75
Different target market, but likely high crossover	1.0
Same target market but different immediate need	2.0
Same target market and same immediate need fulfilled	4.0

Got it? Okay, now, multiply the two together:

Integration Point Factor × Target Factor

= Integration Marketing Factor

Example

Let's imagine you were to approach Starbucks with the following deal: if they let you advertise your company—a service targeted at college students—on their cup holders, you'd pay

(continued)

for the cost of printing their cup holders. This would increase Starbucks profitability by lowering their cost of material, and it would give you some exposure. Would it be worth it?

Let's do the math.

Since Starbucks isn't giving you the name of every customer to whom they give one of your cup holders, this gets an Integration Point score of .75 (Transaction Stream—postsale bundled advertising).

Since Starbucks is a different target market, but there is likely some crossover in that Starbucks has a high student clientele, we'd give it a target factor of .75. (If this deal were only done with Starbucks stores in or next to universities, you could bump that to a 1—different target market, likely crossover.)

Multiply .75 by .75 and this gives you an Integration Marketing Factor of .562.

To help determine whether or not this deal was worth it, you would need to complete the rest of this formula and evaluate the final Integration Marketing Score in relation to: the cost of printing and the relative Integration Marketing Scores of other potential deals.

If, for example, you had other deals on the table that gave you a higher Integration Marketing Score, but didn't require any out of pocket expense from you, you might want to go for those deals instead of this one.

Try this with a number of hypothetical situations, and you'll get it. But remember, this is just Step 1. The final Integration Marketing Score is what really matters.

Step 2: Multiply Your Integration Marketing Factor by the Number of Potential Contacts to Find the Integration Marketing Score

To find your Integration Marketing Score, multiply the Integration Marketing Factor you generated in Step 1 by the total number of people who will be exposed to your UMV.

Since most Integration Marketing Deals occur over long periods of time (that's where the real value of Integration Marketing comes in), you can calculate Integration Marketing Scores over a predetermined time period, thereby reliably predicting your future return.

For example, a daily Integration Marketing Score of 1,000 would translate into a weekly Integration Marketing Score of 7,000, an annual Integration Marketing Score of 365,000, and so on.

Example

To carry on with the earlier example, let's imagine that you will be doing the deal with all of the Starbucks in Springfield (the city where the Simpsons live). All of the Starbucks in Springfield collectively sell 1,000 cups a day. So, you multiply .562 by 1,000 for a *daily Integration Marketing Score of 562.*

Is this a good score?

Well, that all depends. There are no universally good scores or bad scores.

It's like asking "is 72 percent a good score on the final exam?"

In U.S. schools, grades ranging from a high A to a low F are usually handed out on a bell curve. If 72 percent is the highest score in the class, then it's a great score. It would be on the far high end of the bell curve.

If 72 percent were the lowest score it wouldn't be a good score at all.

The Integration Marketing Score works in the same way. It is a tool of relativity. It's meaningless unless compared to other marketing opportunities.

Remember: we're looking for the best deal from a number of options, not simply whether a given deal might be profitable.

Step 3: (An Optional Step, but One That Can Increase Your Predictability) Multiply Your Integration Marketing Score by Any Applicable Modifiers

There are modifiers that can help you hone in on the actual value of any potential deal.

As I said earlier, no strategy can predict or anticipate every possible eventuality. Thus, no list of modifiers that can affect the outcome of your marketing campaign can ever be comprehensive.

I'm calling these modifiers an optional addition to the Integration Marketing Score formula because the person applying these will have to exercise his or her own judgment and use his or her own mental "spin" to assess their value.

But, while these modifiers are therefore more subjective than the others, that doesn't negate their value.

I used to be fond of saying that marketing is "part art, part science, and part voodoo." A successful marketer often has many of the same qualities as an artist or a musician. You develop, from experience, a finely honed sense of what works and what doesn't. Genius emerges from this subjective sense, or "feel."

Having said that, if you want to stick with an objective measure, use the *Unmodified Integration Marketing Score*.

But, these modifiers, if you have the right feel for them, can enhance your predictability.

Recommendation Modifier

There is perhaps nothing more powerful in marketing than the recommendation of a trusted friend. (Except possibly extreme pain.) The *Recommendation Modifier* accounts for that.

But not all recommendations are the same.

Simply select a number for each of the following factors and multiply them together. This will be your Recommendation Modifier.

Notice, that if the reputation of the recommender is low, then naturally the value of the exploit goes down.

A caveat: this formula assumes a positive recommendation. A negative recommendation will, of course, have a stifling impact on your campaign, but you can't plan for that. You certainly don't integrate it into your planning.

Rapport of Recommender with Readers (0.5 to 2.0)

0.5 = Not respected

1.0 = Average reputation

2.0 = Highly respected

Weight of Recommendation (1.0 to 1.5)

1.0 = Positive recommendation

1.5 = Effusive praise

Believability of Recommendation (0.25 to 2.0)

0.25 = Hard to believe

1.0 = Average believability

2.0 = Hard proof presented

Desperation Modifier

The *Desperation Modifier* considers the urgency of a particular need and the number of options available to meet that need.

For example, if a traveler dying of thirst in the desert comes across a single store selling bottled water, you have an absolute maximum desperation factor. If there are multiple stores, or if the traveler isn't all that thirsty yet, the desperation factor diminishes.

Essential to Survival (1.0 to 4.0)

1.0 = Nonessential

1.1 =

1.2 =

1.3 ... and so on ...

4.0 = Life or death

Availability (1.0 to 5.0)

1.0 = Available anywhere

1.1

1.2

1.3 ... and so on ...

5.0 = It's the only available source and there are no substitutes

Pain Relief (1.0 to 10.0)

1.0 = Not relieving any obvious pain (novelty or luxury)

1.1

1.2

1.3 ... and so on ...

10.0 = Relieves extreme pain

As you become more practiced in Integration Marketing, and in using this scoring system, you may very well think of your own modifiers that have a particular applicability to your type of business.

When all else fails, though, stick with the Unmodified Integration Marketing Score. All things considered, it's the most reliable way of making sound business decisions and prioritizing the marketing deals with the greatest profitability potential.

Now, let's look at a few real-life examples of Integration Marketing. I've selected campaigns from diverse industries that are sure to stimulate your thinking.

Some of them will surprise you.

9

Google, Snoop Dogg, and Some Bling-Bling

*Clever Integration Marketing Tactics
Everywhere You Look*

You know how it is: when you're thinking about buying a new car, you start seeing that model everywhere you look.

That's how it is when you understand the mindset of Integration Marketing. You recognize Integration Marketing Deals in various settings, even if the businesses involved don't use that terminology. And, sometimes, you're even a little surprised by the deals you observe. For example, on the home page of IntegrationMarketing.com we have a video of me introducing you to Integration Marketing. Everyone who visits the site sees that video.

We then placed the video on YouTube so, each time the page is opened, we get credit for a YouTube hit.

Did you catch the significance of that? As the video gains more hits on YouTube, it generates more potential for YouTube surfers to find their way to IntegrationMarketing.com.

This is actually a form of Reverse Integration Marketing—instead of using an Integration Point to place an offer, you integrate a technology that opens up new Traffic Streams.

The number and types of deals you can create are literally infinite. Here are a few particularly clever examples that should spark your own imagination.

The Imaginative Relentlessness of Google

It shouldn't surprise anyone that Google would be taking advantage of Integration Marketing. This is a company that leaves no stone unturned in its quest for global dominance.

Here's a minor example (Figure 9.1) that you have probably seen many times with several of Google's Integration Marketing Partners.

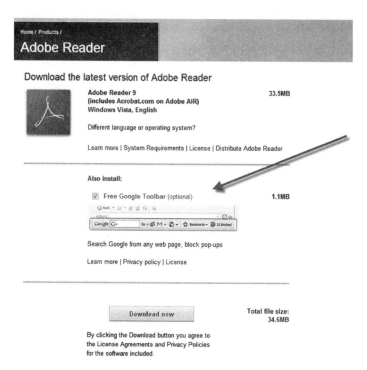

Figure 9.1   One Example of Google's Many Integration Marketing Exploits

As you see, if you want to download the Adobe Reader (by far, the leading product for reading PDF files), you'll be presented with the option to install the free Google Toolbar with your download.

In other words, Google is creating new users out of thin air by piggybacking on someone else's product.

In Integration-Marketing-Speak: Google has integrated its' UMV (the offer to install it's toolbar) into Adobe's Transaction Stream (the process of installing the Adobe Reader).

Is Google paying Adobe for this? Very likely. If they're smart, they are paying Adobe only on a CPA (cost per acquisition) basis. That means, they only pay Adobe whenever someone actually completes a fully registered Google Toolbar download.

This would be a sensible deal structure. It lessens the potential risk for Google and, as you've learned in this book, achieving high return with low risk is the recipe for extraordinary business success.

Even better—Google could barter something that is of little or no cost to Google, but of high value to Adobe.

That's the sweetest deal of all.

Zero risk. High return.

Diamonds Are a Girl's Best Friend

Any guy who has ever gotten engaged has heard "the formula." What you spend on the engagement ring should be equivalent to two months' salary. Anything less is an insult to your soon-to-be fiancé.

More than a few strapped-for-cash gentlemen have no doubt wondered: Who in the heck came up with this formula, anyway?

You may not be shocked to learn that this cultural touchstone was wholly manufactured by the De Beers diamond empire. In fact, it used to be that, while brides expected a ring, it didn't have to include a diamond.

That's before De Beers started a propaganda campaign that transformed cultural beliefs and generated billions of dollars in new revenue.

As part of their campaign, they paid for what is now commonly referred to as "product placement" in feature films.

In the 1940s, De Beers began paying film studios to feature scenes with women wearing diamonds and to reinforce the manufactured belief that a true gentleman gives his lady a diamond engagement ring.

And, of course, once you create the rule—that a diamond engagement ring is required—you can create any corollary subrules to go along with it. Specifically, in this case, the two-month's salary formula.

Some might take a dim view of this kind of cultural manipulation. And, in fact, there are moral and ethical lines in any kind of marketing that should not be crossed. In the case of De Beers, I'll leave that judgment up to you.

For our purposes, we can only appreciate their brilliant use of Integration Marketing.

Translated into our language—The UMV: messages of branding and cultural manipulation that support the sale of more diamonds. The Integration Point: a motion picture.

What the De Beers example shows is the vast range of potential Traffic Streams, and the extraordinary cleverness that can be employed in creating both Integration Points and UMV.

Now, let's switch gears. Let's go from diamond merchants to some of their flashier customers.

Snoop D.O. Double G

Have you ever noticed that rappers will often call out their own names on a lot of hip-hop songs?

Are they just doing that to make themselves feel good?

Nah, these guys are actually genius Integration Marketers.

First, as guest artists on a song, they are integrating their own brand message into someone else's music.

Next, they are smart enough to realize that songs are usually heard without the benefit of a DJ telling the listeners who the artist is. Whenever the song is played, their brand is reinforced.

Are they really thinking that deeply?

Yes, I think so. I have some good friends in the hip-hop industry, and I'm constantly amazed by the sophistication and imagination of their marketing.

It's not surprising that other music genres are imitating this Integration Marketing method. In one of their hit songs, the best-selling country act "Big and Rich" sings, "We were havin' ourselves a Big and Rich time."

And thanks to this kind of marketing boldness, they probably are.

Extra Credit

10

One More Benefit

Integration Marketing as Ecology

I started this journey with the promise of teaching you how to make your business more profitable. I'd like to end on that note as well—but in a way that you may not have considered.

> **Ecology *n*:** The study of the interrelationship of living things and their environment.

For a moment, let's imagine that your business is a living entity.

It does in fact have many of the same features that living things do—growth, adaptation, response to stimuli, and so on—and it lives in an eco(nomic) system all its own.

In biological ecosystems, interdependence determines what thrives and what dies—and how quickly those things happen.

If a species of predators eats too much of their prey, They'll soon start to die off. If these predators were to wipe out their own source of food—which has in fact happened in the past—they would extinguish not only their prey, but themselves as well.

If a species were not linked to others, it could become extinct.

Yet, the world would carry on.

Imagine for a moment that one were inclined to ensure the survival of a particular species. Let's call this species the "Wordia Bird."

The surest way of ensuring the Wordia's survival, if one had godlike power, would be to build an ecosystem in which the survival of other species was linked to the Wordia.

Wolves might eat them, but if the Wordia's droppings are necessary to grow other foods that are essential to the wolves' diet, the wolves could never eat them all. As they started to kill off the Wordia, they too would begin to decline. As their numbers dropped, the number of Wordias they could kill would diminish as well. Balance would begin to be restored.

What does this have to do with business?

Nothing.

Nothing, that is, unless you think that human survival is necessary for business to continue. Then it has everything to do with business.

As you know, we can't engineer various species for interdependence.

We *can*, however, engineer our economic ecosystem for it.

The challenge we face is simple: humans aren't prey to any species but our own. So, the interdependence we must engineer is among ourselves.

The proper tool for this remarkable feat is ...

Business.

Imagine what would happen if we accelerated the growth of ties between businesses around the world.

If your company were dependent on the success of a business partner in Tajikistan, you'd be much less likely to vote for a candidate who wanted to go to war with them.

Further, you'd do everything you could to prevent that war.

You wouldn't care about their religion or customs or language. You'd care about your own survival, which would now be entwined with theirs.

The citizens of Tajikistan, who would now depend on you for their own economic survival, would be equally intolerant of anyone in their country who wanted conflict.

Further, if the people of Tajikistan were dependent on resources from Argentina to produce the goods on which your business relied, both they and you would have common cause in preventing conflicts involving the people of Argentina.

As this web of dependencies and profits grows and becomes more complex, its power grows as well.

It's a simple analysis, but one with ample historical precedent. As the economic ties between countries become stronger and stronger, they are less and less likely to go to war.

These connections can be made most rapidly and profitably through intelligent use of Integration Points.

Integration Marketing isn't just an easy path to business greatness, but one that also engineers a greater chance for human survival.

Integration Marketing is the perfect vehicle for making these connections, because the reward for creating them is potentially enormous for everyone involved.

As business owners, we can accelerate the creation of this web of profitable relationships.

Understand this: it is not our governments' job to do this. It's our job.

This may seem like a difficult task, but there are two things that make it much less daunting.

First, the number of connections doesn't have to be as big as you might expect. Public opinion on such things can be "tipped" with surprisingly small percentages of the population.

Second, by combining the effectiveness and ease of Integration Marketing with the reach the Internet allows you, the process can be accelerated exponentially.

To help with this, we've created a forum where companies from around the world can advertise, free of charge, to find profitable Integration Points and Partners.

You can strike Integration Marketing Deals there with businesspeople from all over the world. You'll find it at

http://www.IntegrationMarketing.com/community.

Whether you are interested in improving the chances of our survival as a species, improving your own life and that of your family—or both, you'll find resources there to help make your business insanely profitable.

In fact, I urge you to go there solely for the purpose of raking in insane profits for your business.

Improving the chances of human survival will just be a nice side effect.

Appendix

Integration Spottings

The mastery of anything comes from two things: observation and practice.

You can get by with practice alone and probably do quite well. However, you may be missing out on new developments that could raise the level of your game. That's where observation comes in.

If you want to master basketball, you'd better hit the court hard—and constantly. At the same time, you'd better keep your eye on the other players, as they might be bringing something new to the game.

It helps to have a peer group that has the same thing in mind. Not only can your peers point out observations you may have missed, but also it turns socializing into a profitable activity.

The Integration Marketing community (forum. integrationmarketing.com) is where you can hang out with that peer group, but we've added another place for you to interact for a more specific purpose:

Integration Spottings—the Official Integration Marketing Blog

http://www.integrationmarketing.com/blog

This blog is not owned by us—it's owned by you.

Integration Marketers from around the world post on the blog any time they spot an interesting use of Integration Marketing.

You're welcome to visit there and swipe profitable ideas at will—that's what it's there for. You're also welcome to post your own Integration Spottings as you find them (so keep your camera handy!)

Here is a small list of some of our contributors I'd like to personally thank. Notice how their contributions to the community have resulted in their UMVs being integrated here? And as Integration Points go—a book—especially one that is likely to be translated into many languages and be spread all over the world—is a pretty good one.

Frank Bauer (of FrankBauer.name)

Hoe Bing (of FlowAcademy.com.au)

Mark Edward Brown
    (of TheMarketing Professional.com)

Tony Funderburk (of TonyWrites.com)

Markus Hart (of FreshWisdom.com)

Shel Horowitz (of FrugalMarketing.com)

Mical Johnson (of MicalJohnson.com)

Allan Katz (of AddictiveEntrepreneurship.com)

Bobby Keating (of Christian-Success-Institute
    .com)

Volker Carl Knoeringer (of HireMyBrains.com)

Alex Navas (of TheMarketingJourney.com)

Diana Sabrain (of SexyFemaleMarketing.com)

Dan Stanley (of SiteSplitter.com)

Dan Wood (or Karelia.com)

We invite you to contribute your very own Integration Spotting at http://www.integrationmarketing. com/blog. If for nothing else, do it because you can shamelessly put your name in lights for the world to see.

A Tip to Ensure Your Post Survives the Review Process: Don't blog about yourself; blog about an amazing case of Integration Marketing you spot out in the world. In the process you'll make yourself famous as the Spotter and get a backlink to your site from your name. That will earn you far more "street cred" and traffic to your site than blogging about yourself will.

Index